T0113193

LETTUCE
LETTUCE
PLEASE
GO BAD

ALSO BY

TIZIANA LA MELIA

and published by Talonbooks

The Eyelash and the Monochrome

lettuce lettuce please go bad

POEMS

TIZIANA LA MELIA

TALONBOOKS

Talonbooks
9259 Shaughnessy Street, Vancouver, British Columbia, Canada V6P 6R4
talonbooks.com

Talonbooks is located on xʷməθkʷəy̓əm, Sḵwx̱wú7mesh, and səlilwətaɬ Lands.

First printing: 2024

Typeset in Avenir
Printed and bound in Canada on 100% post-consumer recycled paper

Cover image by Tiziana La Melia

Talonbooks acknowledges the financial support of the Canada Council for the Arts, the Government of Canada through the Canada Book Fund, and the Province of British Columbia through the British Columbia Arts Council and the Book Publishing Tax Credit.

Library and Archives Canada Cataloguing in Publication

Title: Lettuce lettuce please go bad : poems / Tiziana La Melia.
Names: La Melia, Tiziana, author.
Identifiers: Canadiana 20230590128 | ISBN 9781772016086 (softcover)
Subjects: LCGFT: Poetry.
Classification: LCC PS8623.A1995 L48 2024 | DDC C811/.6—dc23

For Maria

she saw her fingers grating, saw blood flying like carrot flakes, wondered why she imagined blood as part of the salad ...

—DAPHNE MARLATT
"Listen," *Net Work: Selected Writing* (1980)

tutti frutti

NICE POEM

for Sonia D'Alto

Nice, but.

Nice, but there's something, I don't know.

Of the fair rose that grew from a sharp thorn, they
wore pure virgin wool and liked accounting.

Nice, but it's OK, it will be amazing.

Nice, but in this old city *I wasn't in any position to get rid of them.*

Nice, and offers me a Diet Coke and a gluten-free cracker.

Nice, but indebted to kindness.

Nice, she describes herself as a whistle-blower and transcribes
songbirds.

Nice, but having been described myself as sugar and spice and
everything nice, what is she hiding?

Nice, but makes money from plastic and does nothing in particular.

Nice, and composed.

Nice, and forgetful.

Nice is nice.

Nice is a strategy.

Nice enough for supporting foundations.

This is a heavy niceness.

Nice, but one day I'll manage without *you*.

Nice, so I was careful not to upset you in any way.

You may be a saint, and I may be ugly and hairy.

Nice, and chamber music leaks into this room as I try to figure out what kind of nice.

Nice, but I have to remember to ask the question, *do you need the money?*

Over and over, *nice.*

Over and over, I ignore the *but.*

Over and over, it brings me numbness.

Over and over, the nice becomes debt.

Over and over, there is no time to catch up to the nice.

Over and over, *their smiles catch onto my skin, little smiling hooks.*

Nice, and careful not to upset anyone.

Nice, and I am all yours.

Yet I still depended on her, though I did it regretfully.

They seem immune to exhaustion, *airy and in perpetual conversation with the sky.*

At the end of summer, even the flowers notice you are nice as they unpetal.

Nice, I serve you.

Nice, you mine.

Nice, but always watching.

Nice, and exquisite or invisible.

I didn't want any flowers, I only wanted nice, you never brag. I bragged. Basic nice.

Down-to-earth posture with pollen on a shirt and a kerchief around your head.

They'd supported me for so long I was limp.

Nice, but no attention to detail.

Nice, but avoidant.

Nice, but how do we pay the rent?

Nice, and they tell you so much information you trust the nice.

We were chatting about something and instead of *nice* you wrote *mice, mice, mice. I mean nice.*

Nice, but is it easier to be nice when you have an inheritance?

Nice, but need to be nice to live.

Nice, but we can't speak about making a living.

Nice, but it's easy to be nice when you have nothing to lose.

Nice, but this you and we, it doesn't mean you, especially if it's not nice.

Nice, but when I close my eyes *she lays her fire-red tongue under my heel and swallows me instantly.*

I clench the nice as my shoulders hover at my ears.

I collect some nice in the hips and chest and neck.

Nice, like so many things, is complicated.

Erasing sighing nice.

Achingly very agreeable.

I will nice on you.

Nice, and tells you that getting to work for her is a gift.

The opportunity is the payment.

Nice, but I won't tell you the things I feel that aren't nice.

Nice, but I won't dwell so much with my own hypocrisies, and simply point out how nice this is and that is.

Nice, but doesn't have time for negativity.

Nice, and we appreciate the chance to answer your emails all day.

Nice, that they gave us the gift of booking a room at the hotel so we could ornament her ego, *this is my assistant.*

They promised to call me her assistant and put me down as managing editor – just online, though. I wondered why she couldn't put it down on paper but she quoted someone and hummed, *delete is my favourite button.*

Nice as a piece of ice.

Nice, but I needed the money.

Nice, but I needed looser composure.

Nice, but doesn't know that titmice are not mice.

Nice as a mouse not nice like a rat.

Nicely put together.

It's a gift.

Put yourself together.

Days when nice looks micey.

Titmice were not nice when they opened the bottles of milk left on the front steps in England in the 1950s.

One grandmother is nice.

The other grandmother is nicer to brothers.

Great-grandmother twisted her nice hair into a cinnamon bun covered by a scarf. Sorry rhymes with sister in my baby tongue.

I apologize because I'm nice, and you tell me your sister is across the ocean.

Innocent kind of nice.

Self-protective kind of nice.

So nice that she sacrificed her eyes, Lucia, that saint, kind of nice.

KNOTWEED

        Resveratrol is a natural phenol, the blushing stock
    out back. Rub it all over my face
tastes like rhubarb rain.
        Ferulic acid is a high-potency phytochemical
    antioxidant found
in the walls of plant cells.
        How to access the acid is on
    another list to smooth acne scars
we try salad. Wedger
        of negative space. Ruins property value
    rubs bridges
    rips freeways.

        Smoke lace was practised in an atmosphere of
    striving and self-doubt.
    Eclectic
    surgical
    ornamental
    independent
    sentimental
    adaptable
    ogival
    tassa
    sediment

FEED FORWARD

SCENE: Confined inside the room, inside the dream, my grandmother rests in her spot between the fridge and the sofa on a wooden café chair. She describes the objects and routines that both ground a person and transport them. She suggests that I use repetition to create a seamlessness between life and dream. In life, she is anxious to step outside of the kitchen. Outside the kitchen, she rhymes objects with chores. Inside the kitchen, she cleans vegetables, shucks, soaks clothes. She keeps her loved ones close to her, lured to stay inside longer with erotic television programming. Her daughter, her spider, spreads the crocheted bedspread over their legs in the bed as they nap together.

OAKWALKDRONE

for Niscemi

SCENE: *A satellite transmits sounds reminiscent of the addictively popular mobile-phone game saga. Fluttering garbage in the cork oak forest. Birds collect frayed bits and the tinsel of refuse for nests. Night walk to the Mobile User Objective System-4.*

Cork oak forest or yew tree?

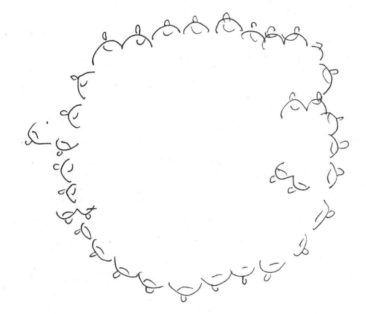

Weird, we didn't eat cake down in the valley where green grass grew

I get one reply
"go to the yew"

So, I visit the cork oak forest to see the trees undo
forced to vibe future

In the mornings a shepherd crosses the fallow
I blow scirocco off the windshield

drive down the street to transport stew
dropping out is what the custodians of the trees will do

rose-coloured sand dropping on morning dew

Will lettuce muss
cursive as the sun ribs?

Late + lone, they drop
drop out, atone

Antennas deter tourists seeking drawers of decorated time

Another sister will monitor blood pressure and heart rates in
exchange for oranges and plays candy

crush. Simultaneously the news catalogues disappearances. Fruit
cooks in sugar

We drink coffee facing the stacks of paper
proof circled by Cicco's abandoned biodynamic garden

Is it hard to participate when you want to disappear?
The fence is an edge of fight-or-flight

I drop "decorative" pink peppercorns in my mouth
making decisions through inherited responses

Eat the decoration kale. Counterpoints to
inherited responses to scarcity. Beans

like some people, creep
Strawberries crawl between shade and light

Life shudders
sink sink shrink

slip, disappear into
cold sugar, to die and return

*shhh*airing pressed shadows
ancient anxious

I put on my sneakers and sneak
while you compose on all fours and remote control

Aluminum antimony arsenic barium beryllium cadmium chromium
cobalt copper gallium gold iron lead

manganese mercury palladium platinum selenium silver zinc
hot on my stomach

Kneading water, seeds + soil represented as marzipan fictions

At the foot of remote (controlled) warfare
lit reveals small troops of mushrooms cast under

moonlight deflect the attention against the effect of gamma rays on
everyone's marigolds

Locked gates are closed step over
click cross tall grass lit by phone flash

decoration is prayer, decoration slows

The second situation
below ankle height

Square pores intersect with
moralizing architectures

portals for rabbits. The first surveillance
mansions insisted on horizontality

Tell me
the abstraction of home in a drone pastoral

on fine hot soil
picnicking

I noticed the skin of the oracle
hard stone fruit

temporary ovens
hillsides teething

Electromagnetic extraction

Everyone using a GPS together
I am still lost

When I want to disappear
I go on airplane mode

The flock moves to the shepherd's guttural trill
hooves split red earth, privately

Gossip makes the world go 'round
but revolutions *shhhhhh* listen to the sore

Grow tenders, wind moves around language mapping geographies
and shared wallows

Treading drags with figures inching, blazing
friction across the oak trees charred shaft

For days the sun kissed all the bottles, plastic or glass or any hollow
container – its kiss melded rock to earth

Gullies with strands of hair stuck to dazzling suckers clinging to
packaging and fruit stickers

Snagging seeds and pollen
Settle in dusty polyester rose

Swimming inside a Sprite bottle, nothing compares
to the self-care moving through air

jellyfish swimming striped candy is created candy blast colour bomb is created colour bomb detonation striped + wrapped blast striped + colour bomb wrapped + colour bomb buttons up release cascades normal switch negative switch time warning load crush candy saga falls level completed level failed cry sweet tasty delicious divine frogtastic sugar crush sugar stars sugar crush fish swimming tickets please all aboard piggy bank feeding piggy bank full enter dream world return reality icing licorice lock is destroyed chocolate is destroyed chocolate is expanded licorice swirl is destroyed licorice swirl hits candy bomb is destroyed candy bomb detonation multilayered icing is destroyed slice of cake is removed cake bomb detonation toffee tornado appears toffee tornado is flying crack disappears sugar chest is destroyed bubble gum pop hit bubble gum pop destroyed rainbow twist destroyed rainbow rapid stops flowing rainbow rapid collect skull appearing skull disappearing skull destroyed bonbon blitz hit booster jellyfish is activated jellyfish is flying to jellyfish eats candy lollipop hit a candy free switch perform free move striped brush brushing sweet teeth eats candy lucky candy is opened bubble gum troll malfunctions chocolate fountains shuffle boosters spawning party booster party popper piñata explosion features conveyer belt moves candy frog selected candy frog eats candy frog full candy frog jumps candy frog lands is flying ufo is activated owl worries owl panics owl falls owl flies to the moon moonstruck is beginning elements jelly clear ingredients spawn ingredients bring down stars sugar star flying sugar star landing sugar crystals explosion sugar crystals flying sugar crystals landing sugar stars celebration stars shimmering clockwise sugar drop spawn candies collect candies conveyer belt is moving during collecting reward sugar

STRAWBERRY TEA DRIVING NOTES

for Lori Spears

Swish pink tea
sip
sip
sip
sip
sip
sip
sip
sip
sip
sip
sip
sip
sip
sip
sip
sip
sip
sip
sip
sip
sip
sip
sip
sip
sip
sip
sip
sip
sip
swallow swoops

swallow swoops
swallow swoops
swallow oops
oops
oops
piss piss piss piss piss piss piss piss piss piss piss piss

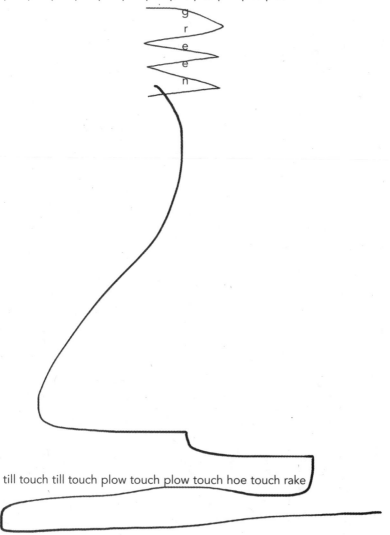

g
r
e
e
n

till touch till touch plow touch plow touch hoe touch rake

sprinkle touch wheel push wheel till spring bush relics sour saga
clip wild strawberries zip halfway rhubarb leaves riding lawn mower
bruising grass fall on knees rub rooms charcoal please vinegar please
applications of glitter bandages two wings on udders the spatter of
white paint dried like sour milk upside down painting a giant till a
chain a rust across seasons draped crust on a car roof denim soaked in
vinegar, rain and rust spritz till patience till abandon grass four seasons
in one shortbread all-purpose flour melted margarine shaping biscuits

NO
SCONES

OUTHOUSE SOS CURSIVE FLIGHT THROUGH THE HEART-SHAPED WINDOW OF THE

wood violets

+

rhubarb-leaf mordant
1 week of saved bath water

=

1 foot of colour

mustard-gold

memory as extracted pigment released from leaves tubes relay matter from the place minerals are taken from and redistributed as figures caressing abstraction

LACE EMBRACE

for Charlott Weise and Franziska Schulz

The psychic ampersand refers
            to the squeezing
of energy
                                                            you know

reshaped

                                    think of those waist trainers
you're literally laced into this thing where you, quote,
                        "Train your waist into being small"
let's say you are in a chair and one chair leg is missing
                        could you still sit on that chair?

trust   try
fall   over
go   over
shifting
            my weight over to one side
            contorting
                        into a   sat in that contortion
                                        snap out
straighten yourself
            out
try
            balance
again
            – swell.
Lace
                        embrace
Corsetless verse
            whipped with a ribbon   relax and bat
                        when I was young /

and bows swish   – foolish / I loved
Siggi & Gerri
                    down like lavish   you drew a
        large cock

                                ponytails   on a gingham cloth

                    – ribs exhale and with   and like the
        clock
head erect / I look down   it will
shape me

        to sud and dew you
        to speak in season and

tie
        down
                forever – here

        A body of ampersands ...   cinched waists

with satin sashes

        married, above the crossroads,   above belly
in flight
                but if he is a Gianni then
exaggeratingly accommodatingly

                retying the

                                &

        makes room for new ties.

A ruff without a support structure wilts

A head of iceberg lettuce left in the heat *uprootedruffs* back to ordinariness

SHH

She sells seashells by the seashore
Sheepish seller in the shell heard,
Cease insurance, by the seashore,
Are seas in hell? Well hell I'm sure,
And the seashells she sells on the shore,
Licked then sold to sci-lore.

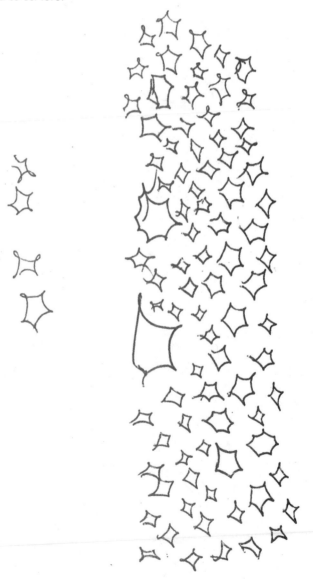

GUIDETTA

Sea guide
to gold
amulet-wearing
Guido beneath
button-up blouse
gold chains
r we
cousins twinkle
my coral
cock laps
across shimmering
sea beyond
shell station
exchange tendrils
of information
at the lip
of the sea
she sells
fossils of trips
to tourists
size science
ear press
rough rows
of cotton
math links
around neck
like freshly
detailed cars
guided towards
unhinged star

I don't follow lace veil across pain and all the vain letting flowers off in the sun I sat on her morals rest in patches burying poems with seeds written among the mushrooms, they follow me letting stress rest for the first time so let's care a stretch and peel stickers off I don't eat you and we let each other be day dew Saturday dues soothing I can love you and barely know you waking up

26

BREATH BOUNCE

Milk lace. I keep getting to this place that is beautiful, it feels like death in the sense that it tightens and summarizes, also expands, I mean, tightening is one way, in the sense that it's a collection of reality into a more purified state almost that is ... that is almost like you have to think about time in a totally nonlinear way I mean, the fractal is so instructive ... it points to the ... cherry tree. It is where herb becomes mind, fractal time, and is assistant in its repetition. It was always the sense of intersecting with this place where, like the tightening moment, where there is something that is happening, and every time we go there, even though you have progressed along your timeline. In this way, that time has passed for you and you go back and it's the same instant. But there are all these buried instants like a Russian doll of reality, where the deeper in you go, the tighter the time gets, and you're intersecting with a different order of time or I almost feel like it's a spiral expanding your life versus tighter. We had just been through the tobacco seedlings and the dormant hogweed and the horsetail and the comfrey and we had just been through the tomato patch. There are all these points in walking back, we walked through the space that was iconic, something iconic. There's all this ... there's all this visual information that seems to consolidate and expand and so when once we ended up in Buffy's library garden, it was like all this visual experience that earlier in the day fed into the thing. But it wasn't just earlier in the day, it was connected, all this deep experience of our friendship and then you and we were in the spiral and then we shared, we shared this kind of telepathic experience, essentially. We're seeing the same colours. The cherry. The plum bushes. We were seeing the same sequence of colours, the same rhythms and sculptures made by the sun. I asked you to lie in the cabbage patch with me that night too, it was obviously the most comfortable place but you felt like your role was to not lie down, the thing about the recurrence of patterns and the amplification and especially with tapping into this young mind-state and the structure of the psyche to me. I've had these experiences but I'm like, yeah yeah ... a final experience in a sense that it's almost like you're being given this chance to build an intuition and the intuition is like so funny the experience keeps knocking you down. There are door walls and it's like, oh yeah oh yeah oh yeah oh yeah yeah yeah yeah yeah yeah … death is like, oh yeah yeah yeah right. *Ha Ha Ha* here's the things, here is the jewel of the experience and look at all its facets.

Dig a hole and get out the hole
Dig a hole and get out the hole
Dig a hole and get out the hole
Dig a hole and get out the hole
Dig a hole and get out the hole

SAY IT WITH FLOWERS

PRAYING
INTENSIVE

baby's breath

love-in-a-mist

cowslip

cupid's dart

dandelion

forget-me-not

snapdragon

narcissus

CAST CALCULATE ARTICHOKE BUG

an air of

FELT

PUPPETS

& RUFFLES

WILL PERVADE YOUR HOME WHEN YOU

GUIDE PLANTS FROM WILDFLOWERS

SQUASH

DISCOURAGING COMPANION ROBBER
Insects with LIVING ALLIES
The basics of watering
MAINTAIN A HEALTHY
FLOWERING
RUSH

Sunset for a Devil

Acidic or alkalkine? What pH means
Taking the TOLERANCE test
Birds, Bats, Toads, & other
sometimes-allies

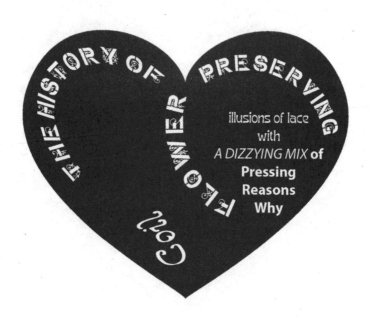

THE HISTORY OF FLOWER PRESERVING

Coz?

PRESERVING

illusions of lace
with
A DIZZYING MIX of
**Pressing
Reasons
Why**

ARE YOU SEROTINY?

HYGRISCENCE (WETTING)

OR

BRADYSPORY (GRADUAL RELEASE OF SEED FROM A CONE
OR FRUIT OVER A LONG PERIOD OF TIME)

OR

PYRISCENCE (FIRE)

OR

NECRISCENCE (DEATH BY PARENT PLANT OR BRANCH)

OR

SOLISCENCE (WARMING BY THE SUN)

PLANT CINEMA

Monday
Tuesday
Wednesday
Thursday
Blink
Monday

SCENE: I walked by my Rose tonight. Walked past pale pale yellow Rose during twilight surrounded by dark foliage and the garden shed. A sprout in the middle of the middle of the path, mostly dirt, two smaller sprouts to the right of the larger sprout. Pumpkin shows up at around 11:36 p.m. Two elusive creeping Vines merge with the blue sky making a diagonal through time. I still have the ability to smell the rain directly from the air. This will die with me.

Inconsideration of molecular fictions

from reality TV to bouillon cubes

pivot

Shake the concentrated vegetable protein in its bottle.

Slender neck and slouch.

Domes of fish and page of bay.

Silver paper wrap cubes of suns boredom compacted for edible pockets.

The work, the repetition.

Empty the cup, dissolve please.

Gorgeous upside-down herb. Rabbit tea.

Soft berry.

Thigh.   Point.

Convenience in the comforting broth.

No tedium   equals no plant cinema.

Fall asleep   to notice   scales of cycle.

Born in the glamorous dirt.

Days of Our Lives in the bodily record of every decision I didn't make for myself.

The country mouse and the city mouse. Sonia added Hamster.

Paris and Nicole and me
Jujube dissolved but remained as yolk dried to a plate.

Egos and eggs, which came first?

Night after night.

Optimism *and* indifference produced delayed dissolve, gleaning
for sugars under the grass.

                                              Shifts the scale.

Bury the economic toil.
How to live with the wilting during a deadline?
... that I sit here, to type pandemically, during this self-vacating ...

I forgot all the doors. Country mouse city mouse.

How to live with the dying during a deadline that I sit here to type
pandemically during this self-vacating.

NEVER WAS A SHADE

Listen!

pigeons on the grass
shadow never was
vegetable
dear and lovable
never was a shade
of any plant
dearer and more lovely
or more sweet
every seven sunrises
I give my blood
she gives her blood
I traded hot wax
for the voice
so what?

Heaven is

open cinnamon!

come over
  to sort
    the spices and pour the spices
      into new jars and eat a slice
        that tastes like air
          with warm spots
            that taste
              like ammonia
                with cold spots
                  that shade

they do
they come
they do

they do
they should
should they
no should

here tonight
in it
take it out of it

say no
to the old spices

I take star anise   I drive

detour to city hall
snap the tiny flowers
type on the phone
flex and pick

drive to my house
pick up the armoire
trade looks

snap more flowers
from my garden
and tender grass

she gives us an octave
another octave
a slice
we kiss the slice
polite and swallow

let's go

let's drive

let's go

wanna go?

let's.

lets

let

let

go

JUICY

visit homespun maidens
touring with velour skins
separating from the gentle man
suited in fleece
baring teeth, blissed
and hissed
"protect you"

nah nah nah
nah

shepherdess in distress
in a two-piece sweat set
sit and mediate on it

meditate on the windfalls
not collected or fermented
rotting plums cemented
on the drama of the winds
blowing the blond grasses
girdled hope
like nah
every decision
depended on
the waist the wind blew
and broke the grass

to revise history as
mere nah
dishevelled
as fear
in aging
Juicy on Paris
the finger swipes the universe
of peach fuzz and hardware

 **BABY**

SCENE: Seeds drying between the pages of a T-shirt on the

porch. Later they are saved in medicine bottles on the ledge.

Time is translated over a heavy table as she feeds the fire.

seeds wrapped   in dried wet wipes
seeds tucked   between newspaper

cut seeds

sometimes
I write
on a timer

there is a movie   being filmed outside

flies crawl up and down

                                        the neck
                                              of the lamp
                                                    near winter

my feet are cold   my heart feels greasy
since I've been here
I am simultaneous and tired
the stove distributes a dry and even heat
the tablecloth is covered in hair, kratom dust,

                                                broken leaves

TRASH LETTUCE

hey
freaky angel

i wrote
what i wanted

a photograph i tore it and put it in a bottle

i broke it
your eyes are
chocolate chipped

when we still
waited

what was it u said
the real housewives said?
about repetition

again?

one month ago
i cooked the trash lettuce

it was tender
and hot

u wrote
"romanticize repetition"

we walked to the top of the hill and lit cigarettes and sticks in the dark
at the rock

i wrote a love letter
in red ink
and left it on the windowsill

and forgot it in the sun

there are so many people in this poem
but it doesn't make you composite
it says time is something romaine
not like the other lettuce
that never
goes bad

lettuce lettuce lettuce

lettuce, please
go bad

not repeat yourself
over and over again
expecting different results
let us
rip off the slimy leaves
and eat

GESTALTING A HYPNAGOGIC BAT DREAM

I am a little bat glossy like licorice, appearing from grey waves while falling asleep. I get a little bit larger, and I glow around my edges an electric purple and begin transforming, becoming multiple and then also like some kind of vampiric figure, which is determined mostly by the big collar of the cloak. Being the vampire now, I am feeling brave, impenetrable in the glossy plastic armour, and am no longer afraid of being glamoured, meaning to be possessed by the vampire's gaze. I morph easily between my forms. Taking and giving energy, tuning into ultrasounds. Echolocation alternatives.

CAESAR

(Trash Lettuce Poem, February 11, 2021)

every new moon
there's a package of hearts
in the fridge

i didn't buy the romaine
but it's there and a bottle of
Caesar dressing

u said she said
it was good, but u
don't cream the leaves
so its own death
comes forward

a month is a long time though
and still
there are parts
of the heart
still
good

no cream, and the world crumbles

the countryside
puns
because death and reproduction
kitten
here
clearly

cream, and crumble

throw away the watch

baby mice fall from the bottom of the engine

teasing time
is easier
if u work
with trees

the heart of this house
is held together with
twist-ties

the cross-section of the heart
is the best part
but every time
u throw it
away

FRUIT SALAD

(Trash Lettuce New Moon Poem, September 5, 2021)

u didn't believe me
until i described the
fruit salad

u (not u) told me u loved it

u smiled and said it was so good

u asked me for more

i believed u
when you smiling
ate the fruit salad

u said u couldn't eat the last one either
even though u smiled and swallowed
in front of my smile

choke assist
sobbing fruit
cut to 1-inch cubes

itchy
tiny moons
of white bread
collectively swallowed
communicates through resting
coins of flour melted over community

u refused to eat the sandwich
the leaf of arugula made u angry

we layered everything u asked for
inside the portuguese bun
plus a leaf

what isn't communicated in all that is said
will block u u u
u grab the last bite u
throw the lettuce out the window

WITH BORAGE

Pick the young shoots, the unopened flower's fat bud

and I knew it
        as a seasonal
                    hold on earth
            held worlds

with furs relaxed

in simmering water

eating the
        dense tissues
                    of closed petals
            under the metallic
sun's grace

CARROTINI

U-PICK TOUGH

FRUIT

GENTLY

BODY FEED

stock's   exchange
spills nutriment over the duvet

fear makes the world go
-aceous give me monosodium glutamate in
Your latte, frothed is
the character   of my love

stiff fingers twist uncooked noodles
into models of sacred diss
cosmic geometry
priestly nonplussed
this history of the
private digestion of sound

        XO
        OXO

love is the occasion for   soup
the present is a fable

wind   wind

reath

over my skin

    forecasts spill
    bring to a boil
    then simmer

clouds settle over
the ice on swan lake
nothing   ripened
the   summer

falls

Midnight chef, oracle
condiment
        wears a tomato crushed
velour   cap
        spills   the
            insides
            out,
        synthesized
        for   worked
        internal   lives
    spin cycle
of growth
    return   the flow
    organized   in   form
        the   home
        (Swiss) factory

I learn on the radio that there is this belief that
Maggi original
soothes nostalgia, ampliflying everyone's taste of home
                                 was the sauce always corporate?
packed into pockets and dissolved later
by workers in transit
or for a fast meal by ma ma afterwork
compressed the vegetable proteins
for watery lives
just two drops over
the nutriment
for corporeal liveliness
even the sun makes produce without aroma
if your fruits are tiny lakes
no amount of tears
equals good taste
with spit and corporeal spill
… I have a question for Maggi …
Who is Maggi?
oracle?   200 ml bottles packed with an internal life

AQUACOTTA

**means cooked water
is a bouillion slip so
herbaceous, verdant, funky
texture smooth or chunky
souping intelligence
fibre figures fib**

rose to rib

cooked water is my memory biscuit

sucked stones for basic mystics